DHARMA IN LIFE'S WAY'S AS KARMA II

DHARMA IN LIFE'S WAYS'S AS KARMA II

GADHADHARAN PUNATHIL

Unity of Humanity under the agesis of God on the yardstick of Dharma or Righteousness.

Contents

Contents

Foreword

" Dharma in life's ways as Karma " is, in reality, a way of living so as to achieve the aim or purpose for which a human being is born as is perceivable specially from Hindutva way of life.. Karma is deeds and activities that a person does for going on in life's journey every day. Dharma is as we all now know is Righteousness or to simply put it purely and simply it's Good or goodness. Dharma in life's ways as Karma is A mean's stipulating a way or rather the only way for a human being enabling the realization of the ultimate goals in a Human being's life. Everyday situations crops up fettering the Dharmic path as is seen from innumerable experiences of humanity's Journey culminating in present times of The Rule of law. These experiences bring in ways adopted and contrived by humanity in adhering to Dharma even in dire chaotic situations. The Author's attempt is to Extricate and bring out these principles so as to make them useful in one's day to day life in accordance with Dharma. Dharma in life's ways as Karma is an endeavor in that line of thoughts....but the necessity to fully unfurl the ways adopted by humans in adhering to Good for the wellbeing, prosperity, and progress in happiness of humanity is so vast it becomes a necessity or rather an imperative Perseverance for the good

of humanity. To add to and substantiate the effectiveness and Good of the already brought out concepts of Righteousness manifestation of " Dharma in life's Ways as Karma II " springs to life. Maybe this will enable and bring about the augmenting of the all-pervading prominence of the concept of " Dharma in One's life's ways as Karma " well beyond any questioning or doubt subserving the common cause of progress of humanity in peace, prosperity and happiness .

Preface

While endeavoring to help decipher the vast experiences of humanity as to the activities, ways and deeds resorted to for adhering to the Dharmic ways in life. It becomes explicit that The more one learns of and about " Dharma in life's Ways as Karma", or deeds and activities resorted to by humanity in different, diverse situations cropping up stultifying the adherence to Dharma in life's Journey. The greater One becomes aware of the infinite unknown necessitating the bringing up of successive endeavors in further trying to unfurl these instances, Primarily intended for helping in salvaging the cause and principles for adherence strictly and completely to Dharma in life necessitating the bringing out and manifesting of " Dharma in life's Ways as Karma II ".

Acknowledgements

"Eshwara Guruveaa". God The Teacher "

Prologue

" Dharma in life's Ways as Karma II " is a continuation of the propositions narrated and brought out for emulation in daily life as is seen in the earlier Book brought out by the author Gadhadharan Punathil as " Dharma in life's Ways as Karma ". In this endeavor, the effort is to bring out further instances molding propositions generally meant for the Good of oneself and humanity as a whole.One has to peruse the expositions carefully and understand the quintessence so as to make it useful indaily life.

CHAPTER ONE

In Continuation of my humble effort to secure adherence to and in Dharma especially in the daily life of individuals, it becomes a compelling necessity to advert to the dispositions of instances that spring up in daily life's ways necessitating the application of principles of Dharmic ways whatever and however ways the situations fettering adherence to Dharma in life's Ways as Karma crops up and are overcome. Signifying and underlining the principles employed in overcoming situations obstructing adherence to Dharmic ways and means. The world takes one to different ways of life to be adhered to so as to bring in blissful happiness prosperity and progress in peace. All profess to be the one and only way to secure wellbeing, welfare, prosperity, and progress in happiness securing success to yonder levels of progress. On a perusal of the different ways espoused by different sects and groups, one will be perplexed and astonishedly confused finding out and choosing the correct way for adherence in which hangs one's salvation. A human being stands like a child perplexed and confused as to which way is the correct way or which way is to be chosen from the diverse selections temptingly available. The choice of the correct way in life's adherence determines a human being both materially as well as spiritually bringing in all-round well-being, progress, prosperity, and peaceful happiness. The need and necessity of present times are the spiritual as well as bodily happiness and wellbeing of the human being as well as humanity collectively. This aspect assumes all the more significance when one notes that, as is espoused in the Author's earlier Book "Dharma in life" , A Human being is the result of coming together of the Particle of God namely The soul and the elements together manifesting as a lively vibrant and efficient human. This all-pervading reality substantiates the necessity for spiritual as well as material well-being and health of an individual so as to make the human being rise to levels of prominence contemplated and stipulated as achievable. These are necessities for a human being to rise par excellence in life fulfilling the obligations and duties of being born as a human being. The cumulative quintessence is that a human being should employ and use the God-given powers and special faculties inherently embodied in themselves such as the powers of intelligence, senses, powers of perception, and reasoning for correctly judging and correctly choosing the path that is to be adhered to in life so as to persevere and achieve the contemplated goals of salvation or realization of God bringing in with it the ultimate in human progress.

Religions are meant as is known to all, to be for securing the good of people Any religion which compartmentalizes human beings into contending groups cannot serve nor will it achieve the purposes for which the Religions manifest. For choosing the correct way for adhering to in life's journey a human being has to strengthen the faculties that enable the selection and choice of the correct way. Only when the faculties of thought, senses, intelligence, perception, and reasoning which guide and provide the attributes for a correct choice work in unison in a correct synchronized manner of functioning will it be possible for a human being to make a choice not only of a correct way of life but also of anything correctly for sure certain success and progress. The capabilities to be prominently necessary for facilitating the choices bring in the reality of the need for synchronized functioning of The Soul and body in unison as hand in glove enabling oneself by endowing vibrant functioning of faculties to excel and surpass oneself to yonder prominent levels of functioning bringing about a balance for easily choosing anything correctly and properly furthering the purpose fo the choice. Only a synchronized functioning of the body and soul will bring about a balanced disposition in a human being enabling one to do things correctly, easily, and quickly catapulting the human being to yonder levels of efficiency and excellence in smartness. This capacity enabling a human being to do a thing or anything correctly, quickly, and easily is called smartness. Smartness is not securing anything or an advantage by deceit lies or misleading others in any way. Securing anything by misleading, deceit, lies, or threatful fear is fraud and is scorned depreciated, condemned as a crime by all and everyone. Fraud vitiates and nullifies as void ab initio even ecclesiastical rights and orders. It is said that Justice and fraud never dwell together. In courts of Justice especially when the working principle is " Fiat Justicia Ruat Caelum" meaning " Let Justice be done Though heavens may fall" , Fraud and Justice are scorned condemned, and declared null and void by any Court, authority, or even a persona before whom it comes for decision. All Judicial authorities and persons before whom these aspects of fraud come for decisions have a bounden duty and inherent implied power with an obligation to brush aside fraud and pass orders correctly and properly anytime anyplace.

In choosing or selecting a correct way for adherence in the daily life of a human being The psychophysical mechanism of a human being assumes paramount importance and prominence. It is the choice of the correct way of life that enables a human being as well as humanity to progress in peace prosperity and happiness. In the matter of choosing one is left to be judgemental and judge himself and The choice determines one's as well as humanity's progress in peace prosperity and happiness. The Holy Quran is held sacred by a large number of Human beings. If one peruses the Quran one finds that Prophet Mohammed the propounded of Islam calling upon all by teachings as of a Religion....." Prophet Mohammed once drew a line and said, This is the path of Faith. Then he drew several lines on each side and said, "On these sides, you may encounter the Devil". But his path of mine is the straight path follow it ".The straight path To God you have to find it This path preaches Tolerance, Humanness, and benevolence. Which is this path you have to find out and choose yourselves. Hadith reported by Abd Allah bin Mas'ud. So comrades the choosing of the correct path attains paramount importance in life's mission. Whatever The choosing of the path to be adhered to in life's ways of Karma is the primary endeavor of any human being so as to bring in success in life's goals and purposes. Choose the way that is espoused by God and is not redundant due to its adverse effects on the Good of humanity. Change has to be necessarily and compulsorily only for good and better not for worse and miseries. Change is the way of nature and an inevitability even in morality. It's said that morality is not static neither stagnant but it's ever-changing. The only requirement fr a human being to accept and adopt change is that Change wherever or in whatever ways, forms and means crops up has to be necessarily and compulsorily Only for good and better not for worse or miseries Otherwise change is not acceptable nor adaptable in life, especially in the life of an intelligent vibrant human being. God our father creator is all benevolent and merciful capable;e of changing even the minutest aspects of life whatever and in however way necessary. As is said in Quran ..declares God as "Rabhul Al Ameen " or the guardian of all in the universe. At Quran 39/53 Quran states.." Don't be disheartened or disappointed about God's benevolence. Surely Allah will forgive all sins . God is all-forgiving and Kind". So comrade's mistakes do happen There is no human being who has not sinned. It's natural and a corollary of being a human being that sins and mistakes do happen but what is needed is that when one realizes that it's a mistake or sin one has to be remorseful immediately resorting to or taking measures for correction and reform and go by the corrected reformed good ways and means so as to achieve the goals. Thus on the discovery of mistakes and sins, one has to be remorseful and correct the mistakes whatever, reform and go on in the corrected ways and means for good showing Repentance and compulsorily taking measures for mitigating the sufferings caused to others by one's mistakes so as to bring in restitution as far as possible. Only these will bring in a disposition so as to persuade and bring in forgiveness in God's mind enabling one to brush off or ward off the hard effects of sins or to at least make the ill effects as molehills when actually its like mountains of adverse bad returns.Its said, " To Err is human but to forgive Divine". So comrades correct mistakes reform adn go on in the correct ways and means so as to get to prominence and achieve the lofty heights of progress in prosperity and peaceful happiness contemplated.

His Holiness Swamejee Vivekananda said," When a person li9ving on a principle commits one mistake others who are not living on a principle commit's hundreds of mistakes". This if accepted brings in the necessity of a human being living on a principle or concept as Good in life so as to see to it that life becomes a path of success of progress peace and happiness. Actually, life is a blessing the difficulty is to find a way to live life so as to make it beautifully Good and happy. Anyone who faces life's situations seriously has to confront this situation at one time or another in life's ways. Think of it When one does something bad and necessarily gets back in the same coin as is stipulated by Karma Yoga substantiated by consistent and realistic scientific principles. One becomes aware that it's not good to do bad things in life. One desires to get something that belongs to another and cannot be got in good ways Unfortunately blinded by the desire to somehow get this thing this person goes about doing bad things in order to appropriate this desired thing and somehow gets it. Of coursc, it is tr5ue that the thing is in the hands of the bad doer but it is also a reality that In spite of getting the desired thing the bad doer's conscience will always haunt and prick him taunting him always thinking of the bad ways employed to get the thing is not meant for him. This is an instance of life becoming miserable in spite of getting the desired thing in bad ways leading to remorse, miseries, and unhappiness in spite of having the desired thing in hand. When failures spring up in life these bad doings crops up as causes of the bad doings leading to unhappiness and agony. On the other hand in spite of awaked situations and ways, one does nothing bad in getting things or achieving positions even if some failures or unhappiness ensures one can be satiated that after all I have not committed anything bad So these unfavorable situations coming up must be the wilful doing of one's adversaries, therefore, Why should I worry, Thereby wiping out the unhappiness bringing in a peaceful and balanced disposition in life. This is also a reality in situations One does all that one is capable of doing but could not completely save the other from perils ...In spite of such failures, one can be at mental peace thinking that after all I have done all that I am capable of doing as a human being in that awaked situation and be absolved of unhappiness. So comrades by Good deeds and activities one gets mental peace and happiness wherein bad deeds bring remorse trauma and unhappiness, especially by the pricking of one's consciousness. In conclusion, one can safely say that Good deeds bring in mental peace happiness, and progress in life. So the choice for happiness peace and progress depends upon what one does or decides to do . Thus the choice of a principle in life for doing things or anything for living life has profound effects on the ultimate outcome in life's ways bringing in a situation that it's better to be on the side of Good in every situation. Even if happiness is pitted against the good it's better to be on the good side. Take the instance of Narcotic drugs. One gets a sort of illusory happiness on taking drugs giving a sense of illusory happiness in using drugs or other like substances and habits. Happiness is not real happiness its like happy situations for a little bit of a time after some time leading to melancholic dispositions causing trauma and cynical behavior. This shows clearly that choosing to be on the Good side or Good way that is not in any way redundant due to its adverse effect on the Good of Humanity is best for anyone and everyone even if it's against happiness. When two ways or say many ways are there all having some bad effects the best way is to choose the way that has the mildest or trifling ill effects. This is the Righteousness or " Dharma in life's ways as karma".

Confronted with a situation of making a choice of a purpose or principle to be adhered to in life's ways it's better for oneself to adhere to the choice of being on the side of Good rather than taking the bad side and be traumatized in unhappiness later. In an akin life situation long back I chose the concept " Believe in the powers of Good, help all who are good and trying to be good ". Any choice can be made as to its a free world with all human beings being endowed with freedoms universally recognized adopted and propagated with a duty on all to recognize and give effect to these freedoms as human rights. Any human being regardless of caste, creed, race, color or religion, or otherwise differentiated are basically held to be equal and treated equally as a human being with all freedoms and protection. These individual freedoms are available to all collectively as well as to any individual human being. But these freedoms do not give any right to anyone to exercise these freedoms in such a way so as to cause harm and negation of others' rights either collectively or individually. When individual; freedom is pitted against collective general well-being,

Unity, safety, and security of humanity individual freedoms should yield so as to be amenable to reasonable restrictions enabling the prevalence of general well being and welfare of humanity. The same goes for in the case of the Nations of the world. The concept that nations or people cannot interfere in other nations' affairs has a reasonable exception that in case of common problems faced by humanity anyone and everyone has a right to raise their voice so as to enable eradication of the malady of the problem or disposition causing miseries, harm, or in any way hampering peaceful existence progress and Good of all or say Humanity in general. Every individual has a right to freedom of speech and expression of one's thoughts and views mainly intended for securing the good and progress of oneself as well as others bringing in the incidental rights of socializing with friends and fellow human beings. This is so especially because human beings are social beings living in interdependent societies and families. These freedoms do not give an unfettered right of speaking falsely ill of others or rumor-mongering saying that it is their opinion causing hatred and harm to oneself as well others. No one has the right to spread falsities and unreasonable views so as to bring in contempt, derogation of prestige, and credit of others. Speach impinging the credit to others can be taken out of crime only if it's true and meant for the general good of the public or humanity in general. This concept is known as Justification by Truth and in purpose.No one can be besmirched with falsities and lies merely because someone thinks that the other is like that, especially without any reasonable reasons. Reasonable reason means that real incidents and instances should be there justifying one's assumptions and speech. When an opinion is expressed by a human being on another person either through media or otherwise it should be capable of being justified by Truth and also that it's necessary for the public good. This is the sole and only guideline or mandatory criteria for media reporting and public speeches, and utterances, especially in public places otherwise it will be a violation of humanity's right to information and right to choose correctly, especially in democratic universal franchise elections. Freedom of information means The freedom of an individual and all to get truthful correct information. This is a cardinal freedom in modern times wherein all depends on the individual taking a correct decision in choice after judging situations and problems. Even the success of Democracy and the good of people depend and hangs on the choice of the universal franchise of people correctly on truthful information of the contending candidates. Only truthful information about the qualities and drawbacks of candidates will enable the people to make good decisions in choosing their representatives so that only good and happiness will ensure. When all falsities and untruths are allowed to be carried and propagated through the media without any criteria as to how freedom of speech is to be exercised information received will be falsities without any truth in it transgressing the Right to information of individuals making it unworthy of being acted upon to augment one's as well as others interests and wellbeing in general.In these circumstances of uncontrolled speech and publication of falsities, People won't get true and correct information so as to exercise their choices correctly making their choices defective bringing in chaos and corruption as is desired and intended by a few people who control the media and news facilities t3ending to perpetuate the sabotage and ravage of humanity's progress in peace prosperity and happiness.These are instances of Dharmic situations cropping up and solutions in the everyday activities, acts, and deeds of human beings in their journey of life. Here one finds the individual's freedoms pitted against the collective general Good, well-being, security, Unity, happiness, and welfare of humanity necessitating the solution of reasonable restrictions on individual's freedoms in the interest of the general Good of humanity.These realities for curtailing the unfettered freedoms of individuals are the results of Good leadership's efforts to see to it that the General Good of humanity prevails over mean unfettered individual freedoms. It's said that unfettered unguided freedoms tend to become despotic as is inevitable from the fact that The two exceptions to the applicability of the all-pervading theory of Economics, " The Law of diminishing Marginal Utility" are Money and power. The law of diminishing marginal utility stipulates that a person who eats one orange will get a great utility than when he eats the second the utility will diminish a little.This decrease will go on and on until eating another orange will not be of any utility to the individual. This utility law applies to all desires and yearnings except Money and power. Unfettered freedoms are the power to do anything on the whim and fancies of the individual leading to corruption of one's ego and sliding to despotic evil attitudes for snatching anything fanciful for oneself without giving any consideration to others' good, rights, and welfare resulting in despotic hypocrisy and despots endangering humanity as is seen in case of persons like Idi Amin, Hitler, etc necessitating Good leaders bringing the concepts of reasonable restrictions on freedoms of individuals in the interest of General good of people and humanity as a whole. These austerities spring up in order to preserve general good wellbeing, welfare, security, safety, peace, prosperity, and happiness of the people as a whole or general public. People who are in control and capable of preserving for the good of human striving and persevering for the good of humanity judging the situations in the light of true information as to situations and dispositions decide that for preserving the good of humanity reasonable restrictions are necessities. Good Judgements and decisions come only from people who are honest, impartial, and open-minded with an inclination to go by reason and natural justice. Or to put it briefly only Dharma brings in decisions good for the people's progress in peace, prosperity, and happiness. People with Good ways and means for achieving anything and everything in life turn out to be judgemental as a corollary for deciding which is good and possible. Being judgemental is part of life and cant be avoided. Every day one gets up from bed first one decides whether to sleep a little more than yesterday and does so so it's judgemental..Then after getting up whether to go to the latrine first or brush teeth ..this also brings in the judgmental factor to take decisions this goes on in every aspect of life's ways.No meaning in condemning everyone for being Judgemtnal and deciding for their betterment good and progress as well as of others.So goes life's ways. Every second every minute and every hour one has to be judgemental and decide as to which way or what has to be done taken or attempted. Success in life and proceeding on becomes completely dependent on one being Judgemental and deciding correctly.Being

Judgmental is for ones own good and is Dharma in life's ways as Karma.

Another cardinal aspect which arises for introspection in life's ways as karma is the attribute of Anger. Anger signifies that the Human being or person do not like the given situation or that he is belligerent toward the situation. Anger aggravates on further provocations leading to direct clashes leading to harm destruction and death As a corollary when one sees another angry one has a duty to cool off or taper off so as to reduce the explosive situation from becoming catastrophic. These are instances of people getting angry for unreasonable, antihuman attitudes and purposes When people get angry for these unreasonable, not good situations, purposes, and dispositions we see others not cooling off or tapering so as to defuse the awkward situation ensuing confrontations, clashes, destructions and ravage. In any circumstances, if one has to avoid explosive situations it is a necessity that one has to learn to control anger so as to enable oneself to cool off when faced with explosive situations and dispositions opening a way to turn off an immediate confrontation capacitating oneself to take up the matter elaborately later on if necessary after equipping oneself and getting ready to face the situation in whatever manner necessary. This controlling of anger becomes a compulsory necessity, especially when facing an opponent who is much more powerful and mighty for otherwise, one will get into an awkward and dangerous situation of even being getting obliterated. Thus controlling anger is a necessity in all situations. Anger even though a necessity for expressing the utmost dislike and aversion to a given situation expressed it is advisable to practice control of anger in all and every situation so that one or everyone will be able to deal with the not good situations in a proper manner appealable to senses in accordance with the common course of human conduct and natural; course of events thereby making the situation good for all. In the Hindutva exposition of the Divin logic of Bhagavat Geetha made by The incarnation of God, Bhagavan Sree Krishna to Arjuna who symbolizes human beings .It is brought out :

Krodham bhudde samoha
Samoha Smrete Vibrahama
Smrete Vibhrama tat bhudee nasoo
Bhudee nasoo pranasyathee .
meaning : Anger leads to distraction
Distraction to discomposure
Discomposure to loss of intelligence
and loss of intelligence to destruction and death.

Manifestly perceivable is the necessity of controlling one's anger in all situations as unavoidable for enabling one to strive for the good of oneself as well as of all. Anger as is seen like other attributes God bestowed, is a necessity enabling humans to strive forward in life's ways pushing aside bad and embracing good propelling humanity to yonder levels of progress in peace.

Dharma in life's Ways as Karma when considered with respect to Governing one's family, or say District, State, Country or the world itself brings in the cardinal yardstick and compulsory necessity of namely "The Good of the people" which is the same as Good of The Country. The Modern concept of Democracy is the in a thing that is espoused as The rule of the people by the people for good of the people having its basis in the universal adult franchise. Here also one finds the common goal of The good of people as the yardstick for perseverance as an activity or Dharma in life's ways as Karma. The common Goal of people's Good is Dharma bringing in the reality that in Governing The District State Nation or the world at large the mandatory measure scale is Good for people. This Governing of the people by the people for the people is called Democratic politics establishing beyond any reasonable doubt that Politics is actually Striving or preserving for the Good of the People " When the striving or persevering is for the state it's state politics otherwise as the case may be when one strives for the good of the whole world its world politics.In politics also one sees Dharma as the yardstick or common baseline to be achieved. If one goes back in History it is obvious that the modern concept of Democracy was made practical in a way as long back as much before 700 B C in Hindutva India by the Emperors of Mauryas. This is long back even before The Roman empire that democracy was practiced in a sense that In THe courts of Hindutva kings a council of ministers was there to aid advise and help the King in all matters of governance of The country intended to help secure the best available for Good of people. The King was like the President giving his seal of approval to all proposals and ways after elaborate discussions in the council of Ministers Or Rajya Sadas (King's court) before approval and putting up for King's approval with the only difference that The office of the King was hereditary. The nine gems in the court of Emperor Chandra Gupta Vikramaditya, chosen only on the basis of merits of high intelligence and capabilities to strive to preserve and suggest ways and measures for people's good were or are the best examples of democratically chosen eminent personality working for the Good of the general people found in the Golden age of Hindu India under The Emperor Chandragupta Vikramaditya ..Emperor Asoka, etc .keeping the light of Humanity'scivilisation high and burning Perserving form the Good of the people in all circumstances. Even in selections for every cadre and matters, one finds that Dharma or righteousness is the cardinal factor emphasized given importance and personified having cardinal factor having significance in Modern day to day situations bringing in the reality that it is Dharma which assumes importance in everyday life of all and everyone whether it is Politics. Economics or other private personal affairs.It is the adhering to Dharma that brings out the excellence in a human being's life capabilities and capacities catapulting Human being to lofty heights of yonder progress prosperity and prominence.Dharam is a concept safely adaptable in managing the Political, Economic, and social situations and services of Nations as well as the world so as to secure The Good prosperity and peaceful progress of humanity. Dharmaism is a concept safely adaptable in managing and administering the socio-political and economic spheres of a Nation and The World at large so as to ensure The Good, welfare, wellbeing, happiness .prosperity, and peaceful progress of the people.Innumerable social political economic concepts have been tested by Humanity for ensuring the prosperity and peaceful progress of humanity from times immemorial namely Autocracy, Theocracy, Marxism, communism, Capitalism, Socialism, Mixed Economy, etc Unfortunately almost all have except mixed economy resulted in failures Capitalism is the practice prevalent in the United States Of America which has resulted in a concentration of wealth, say about eighty percent of wealth being controlled by a few Billionaires leaving the vast majority of common man alien to wealth and wellbeing in prosperity. There are about some three thousand multi-billionaires in The world and think of it they control the majority of wealth leaving just a few percent to the rest of the population of say altogether seven billion or so These bring to light the enormous disparity and inequalities rampantly persisting even going to the extent of denying large sections of society even the capacity and capability to afford proper meals daily pushing them below poverty line thereby inducing an introspection as to the need for some measures to see to it that all are equally provided the basic necessities of life so that they can well be assured of their means to live and concentrate on more higher levels of thinking for necessities and inputs ensuring the progress of humanity to yonder levels contemplated. The United States of America does not come within the first fifteen nations of the world wherein the best living conditions exist bringing about real Good progress and happy people.If one adopts sustainable happiness as a yardstick for ascertaining Nations progress it manifests that it is the sustainable happiness of The Nations people that determines the National progress and prosperity. It's the flamboyant sustainable happiness that imbibes and permeates into all sectors of the population of a Nation that determines its prevalence and prominence as a progressed nation. People's sustainable happiness is the only compulsorily necessary measure scale that can be employed and adapted to measure the Progress of a Nation among Nation's. What progress sis ti when forty percent of people or say at least ten percent of the people going hungry and in difficulties, as they cannot afford proper meals daily even though The Nation sends people to moon and space as tourism catering to the elite super-rich Dandy snobs coming into prominence or attempting to rise to prominence flaunting their richness and disgusting behavior impinging upon and blatantly ravaging the good of humanity.The super-rich intoxicated by wealth and their eagerness to do whatever they just desire even if against Dharma, law and ordinary course of human conduct abusing their wealth resort to Satanism and Satanic cults contriving and bringing in a way to do anything that is forbidden as not Good for humanity and escape by abuse of wealth corruption and power thereby causing untold miseries to ravage and wrecking humanity's general prosperity peace and progress in happiness. Adharma in life's ways as Karma is the only cause of concern bringing in turmoil ravage and decadence pushing humanity to dark ages retarding progress and wreaking havoc in ravage and miseries. Satan is the Angel of evil and Adharma. Satan is part of God's scheme of arrangement of ways of the world and is a necessary evil.God created Satan so as to oversee the destiny of Evildoers and Adharmees.Adharma kindles and ignites Satan's attention as Dharma kindles and ignites God's focus on one. Satan overtakes and permeates adharmic and pervades thereby making the doer his own Think of it comrades People who endear God by persevering in adopting Dharma in life's ways as Karma will be taken to God's fold and facilitated in Heaven with the promise of sustainable blissful happiness in immortality as is explicit from all religious teachings and realities experienced by humanity. Heaven is God's abode where only sustainable blissful happiness in immortality prevails and is reserved for God's own human beings.Adharmis or evildoers will be endeared by Satan necessarily taking them to his abode namely Hades or hell wherein putrification decadence miseries agony pain and sufferings prevail.The quintessence is as any other Angels Satan also does Satan's duty as in enjoined by God and cannot be obliterated by anyone except by God if and when wished or desired. There is no war between God and Satan.The war is only in people or humanity's Karma in daily life. The war is in the decision-making process and adherence of persons as to whether they should adopt Dharma in life's ways as Karma endearing God or Adharma in life's ways as Karma endearing evil and letting Satan overtake oneself and pervade pushing oneself to perils and miseries. Eve endeared to Satan and then persuaded Adam to go by Satan's lies and deceitful ways pushing humanity to perils.So it's the Judgemental decision-making process of choosing good or bad that is the war or armageddon going on always in all human beings against Satan. God's prevalence in yourself dissipates Satanic qualities banishing Satan from ourselves otherwise Satan. It's all nonsense and fallacies that God will come or send someone to wage the last war subduing Satan and chaining him etc The war comrades are still on and being fought in ourselves and only ourselves. Even The Holy Bible says that Satan cant be destroyed completely. Satan is an indestructible Angel of evil and manifests and gets strengthened on or in evil doings. The power is within Humans to determine their destiny God only takes sides and leads with benevolence and forgiveness to the worthy. Satan is no competition for God nor is any competition or compromise necessary.It's the human beings for whom Satan is a competition and these competitions have to be won by human beings with God-given or bestowed powers of intelligence. senses, perception, Doubt, and reasoning streamlined by one's Dharmic ways of life as Karma.A human being is created in God's own resemblance says Holi Bible thereby bringing in an implication and inference of God-given powers enabling a human being to control and.Its the choice of ways of life and activities in the life of a human being that determines destiny. One has the capacity and capability to choose bad as well as good. Its the choice and adherence to good ways that assume importance in determining the destiny of oneself as well as others.As one's Father provides facilities support and inputs to oneself so as to enable one to come up in life surpass and come to prominence in life Our creator God provides all that is essential for Rising above oneself surpass oneself and reach upto God in ultimate progress.So comrades eschew and rid oneself of qualities that make oneself a schadenfreude. Holy Quran says or addresses God or Allah as " Rabhul Al Ameen" meaning The guardian Father of all in the world espousing and buttressing the concept of God being The Father of All in the world interested and concerned in the wellbeing and good of all.The interplay of natural forces arranged and arraigned permanently inconsistent ways determines one's destiny fueled and guided by one's Karmas in life's ways.Satan is nothing and can't even scathe or brush with us except when we by our deeds allow Satan to dominate or brush on us and take us to hades.

There is no one who has not committed any mistakes.It's futile to worry about the mistakes and past evil inadvertently committed. God-given posers of senses, intelligence, perception, and reasoning help us to detect decipher and know of the mistakes and use our or ones conscientiousness namely The power and voice of soul to correct mistakes and move on strictly adhering to the ways of Dharma. It is said that "To Err is human but to forgive Divine". When one realizes and becomes aware of the mistakes inadvertently committed one's conscience arises in remorse yearning to undo the wrongs by correcting the mistakes reform oneself and move on in Dharma. Another unavoidable necessity for mitigating the ill effects of adharmic deeds is to do everything possible to mitigate the sufferings caused by these wrongs to the levels possible mainly by helping the victim or victims to get back to the position as was when no wrong was committed. Restitution of the victims as far as possible is a compulsory necessity so as to mitigate the ill effects of sins and wrongs. These are measures that ignite the power of godliness enabling the making of a molehill the mountain of ill effects thereby negating the harmful effects and consequences of adharmic activities on the doer.Even if one has committed mistakes and inadvertently done adharmic acts harmful one has to on coming to know of the mistakes repent in remorse, reform, restitute and go along with the Dharmic path and ways so as to enable one to scale yonder levels of progress in peace. The quintessence manifests that one's destiny is determined by ones choosing the correct ways and Karma in life's ways.There is no meaning in lamenting that destiny is inevitable and there is no meaning in trying to prevent destiny or fate. One is to a greater proportion responsible and the architect of one's destiny except when confronted and saddled with natural calamities bringing about unfavorable situations and dispositions wherein all suffer to an extent due to the mistakes and evil doings of some.These mistakes of oneself affecting all mandatorily bring in the collective responsibility of a human being to not do anything that will bring in harm to others also Making any human dutybound to raise his voice to common problems faced by humanity as a whole irrespective fo the nation or position one is in intended to get these maladies eliminated negatived and corrected enabling Humanity to surge forward in progress prosperity, peace, and happiness.On an evaluation of these dispositions, one comes to the reality that even The United Nations Organisation has been brought about so as to realize achieve and make practical the purpose and goal of Good of humanity in General.The economic policies and concepts that is being adopted are mainly with the aim of providing humanity a means and way so as to achieve economic Political and other equalities and freedoms so that humanity will surge forward in prosperity peace and happiness. All these collective efforts by great nations of the world are mainly intended to secure the welfare and good of humanity or say the about eight billion population of the world especially giving accentuation to basic equality of human beings as humans. Dharmaism is a socio-political-economic concept practiced by Hindutva societies long back so as to bring about the Good of people basically in spite of yawning differences in capabilities, capacities, aspirations, and attributes considering humanity united in diversity.This concept of Dharmaism was rampantly practiced by Hindu Emperors long before these were known to others bringing about the Golden age of Hindu India. It is really encouraging to note that even in ancient times of Hindutva rulers like

Chandra Gupta Vikramaditya, Emperor Asoka, etc there were even hospitals for animals, rest houses for travelers, and food shelters, and clothing for all considering all humans as basically alike being humans. All that is good for the good and progress in peaceful happiness were accepted adopted and practicalized so as to bring in the desired results of the Good of humanity. Dharmaism, as can be perceived, is accepting adopting, and practicalizing all that is necessary to achieve the Good of humanity irrespective of whether its macroeconomics or microeconomics whether it is capitalism, socialism, Mixed economy, or others. The only criteria for acceptance and use as the practice is the Good of humanity or the general public.Here one finds that it's the human being who is important all amenities and facilities including gadgets etc are meant to secure the well being and good of human beings.In socio-political-economic concepts that concept which gives importance and equality to human beings basically has to be accepted and others eschewed. Only this will secure the intended results of Good of humanity espoused and professed by Great organizations brought about by Nations of the world meant for securing the welfare and wellbeing of humanity.All these one finds are intended to bring in sustainable happiness to human beings. The criteria is sustainable happiness brought about by the natural course of human conduct and natural course of events and dispositions and not unnaturally brought about happiness adharmically achieved by perverted paradoxical acts and activities. Unnatural activities and deeds incessantly imposed and bringing in habits which on continuation, later on, become addictions necessitate medical intervention so as to bring back the individual to mainstream society.In these maladies traumatizing society one finds that its Dharma in life's ways as Karma that plays a major or primary role. Adharmic happiness is not sustainable happiness as is evident from the happiness that a psychotic killer gets from killing, A rapist gets from rape, a drug addict gets from drug addiction, Paelopide gets from these heinous acts, Same is the happiness one gets from anything unnatural and adharmic ways tending to degenerate and ravage humanity and humanness making humans inhuman diabolic schadenfreude. Laws brought into being by trial and error of thousands of years of experiences time tested meant for the good of humanity intended to nip paradoxical perversities gnawing off humanness should not be interfered with except after a thorough evaluation and consideration of all aspects of the malady otherwise this will bringing catastrophic repercussion of calamites, blizzards, and decadence. History is witness to these necessities as is coming in with gay legalization. If one go back in History one finds that gay sex was legalized in 100 A D by Rome the result was catastrophic and eventually pushed the world to dark ages with ravage and decadence. It was only in the middle ages or medieval period that humanity realized the ill effects of gay sex legalization and after considerable efforts made gay sex punishable with death when caught. One has to have common sense and prudence to think of these and answer to oneself...Why did humanity after the legalization of gay sex in 100 A D make it punishable with death when caught in the renaissance period of medieval ages. Any prudent person with common sense will unhesitantly say that it's the ravage and ill effects that these unnatural maladies brought about that brought about these changes for good of Humanity. Nowadays one finds that gays are legalized merely by some Judicial officers of The Supreme court of the United States of America says five Judicial officers sitting together as a bench for deciding the gay issues. Nothing wrong in it prima facia but The paradox is that if one peruses the matter minutely it's itself illegal and amounts to striking down the basic structure of administration of Justice by The Court of Justice itself manifesting in fraudulent orders arrived at by going against and suppressing the concept cardinal to and in the administration of Justice namely " No one shall be Judge of his own cause". This brings in a mandatory law that no one who is interested in the issue for a decision cannot be judge in the decision rendering process. Here in the United State of America Supreme court, one finds that all Judges except one was interested in the gay issue in one way or another rendering the judgment deceitfully fraudulent and non-est as void ab initio rendering the order nullity. These repeated to make gay rights nowadays. Think of it anyone who is gay if looks back and will find that when this guy was a child innocently going about playfully some perverse person befriended the child and abused her or him. This child out of shame and fear or because this guy admonished the child not to tell anyone did not tell anyone and this abuse continued The child thing that this was like that acquired a way for these abuses and started doing it with other children bringing in a habit and consistently pursuing of these perversities brought about an addiction and manifesting a hardcore gay. This is a group brought about by illegalities and abuse how can this perverse illegal group be given equality with natural genders and treated equally. This is transgressing the concept of that only equals can be treated equally. It's the adharmic activities that bring in catastrophes and ravage of humanity necessitating stringent actions to stymie the sliding of humanity to certain decadence and perils. Gratitude is the hallmark of humanness. Oly humane deeds and activities get gratitude. Adharmic activities brings in censure and ingratitude ensuing in chaos and decadence. In these aggravating adverse circumstances, it was best for a straight thinking Judicial officer or anybody interested in the Good of humanity to cause an investigation into the affairs and ways of the gays as to the means adopted by them for achieving their objects and aims and as to what is their aims and goals with special emphasis to gays treatment of children and the children's rights If its found that gays aim arent Good for humanity or that its to make all gays in whichever ways possible naturally it infringes on the others rights and freedoms transgressing the concepts of equality on the basis of which gays claim rights.In spite, of having world-renowned organizations like the United Nations Organisation's no impartial investigations by crack honest investigators with respect to gays affairs ways and aims are not even attempted or ADVERTED TO IN ORDER TO BRING UP TRUE FACTS AND INFORMATIONS FOR DUE CONSIDERATION IN MAKING LAW's FOR HUMAN GOOD AND WELLBEING. This lethargy in spite of a report by the children's commission of UNO that abused children has a tendency to become rapists and criminals in later life if properly not treated by psychologists' intervention.Take this in the reality that God created Males and females for copulation and for being consorts and partners in life ways so that the combined effort will result in the good for humanity. Holi Bible says God created Adam and finding Adam lonely created Eve out of the rib of Adam signifying the fact that eve is to be part and parcel of Adam and vice versa. This natural course of events and human conduct brings in a compulsory necessity that it's the males and females who are to from families coming together as a unit so that humanity's progress in peace prosperity and happiness is always assured. It is the besmirching of families that bring in catastrophic disintegration of humanity's progress and well-being. Whatever God creates is best and humans impinging upon natural ways of nature brings in harmful effects. The creation of coming together of males and males for sex and vice versa females and females for sex brings in the ravage of pandemics and cynical dispositions ravaging thew humanity. Think of it most gay homosexuals go for anal sex. The anus is for ejecting the waste of the human body and not an office for sex. Then sperm is held sacredly by the D N A intelligence engineering of human cells as it ignites a new life and all cells are programed to preserve sustain and protect sperm so as to facilitate anew life. Naturally incessant anal sex and deposit of sperm create a flutter in the cells bringing about a similar paradoxical effect in the human body and brain as a whole and the cells of the anus trying to create a vaginal like situation seen from the change in the pelvic structure and rectum of incessant anal sex protagonists This brings in a cynical crazy behavioral pattern in these persons which can be detected by mere watching.Watch them turn cynical and diabolically sadistic when their overtures are repelled No wonder in Roman times and later persons were seen as abusing dead bodies so as to realize their unnatural sexual gratifications. Add to this the finding of the experts that H I V is rampant among homosexuals. Why freedom should be given to some ways creating crazy and cynical human beings hazardous to the health of all. The wrecking of family life is rampant and practices by gays they do give much to the noble relationship of male and female as is enjoined by God they allow their mates especially wives to have sex with even father and others A similar report was there on Facebook posting in my profile wherein the gay's wife was forced to have sex with his father and brother for begetting offsprings. Thus the conclusion that what is enjoined by God creates progress prosperity and happiness whereas interfering and meddling with God's dictates brings in ravage pandemonium miseries, agony, and decadence, In conclusion, one can safely say that its the male and females who are entitled to come together as a family and help humanity to surge forward in happiness peace prosperity and progress to yonder levels contemplated. It is with this in mind that Hindutva sanyasis were entitled to marry and have families in their journey of the quest to Perceive necessities from nature and Godliness meant for the good of humanity. Merely because sanyasis are engrossed in the quest for enlightenment and the good of humanity that does not mean that they cant marry. Actually, a human being is the coming together of the particle of God and the elements. Thus a human being has a body as well as a soul brin9ingi in the necessity for a human being to cater to the needs of the soul as well as body. The body needs nourishment sex care comforts etc whereas the soul needs only righteousness as its nourishment and exercise. A human being has to cater to the needs of the body as well as the soul in a Dharmic, righteous way so as to enable oneself to achieve the contemplated goals. If one peruses Hindutva concepts and way of life one finds that almost all Sanyasis including Valmeke who wrote Ramayana married and had families so as to aid and buttress their quest and endeavor for the well being of humanity. Even NASA of U S A is spellbound as to how the ancient sanyasis knew of the Sun's chant "Aum". It's only in the Brahmacharya state of attaining sannyasa that one is not entitled to marry and have sex. No, wherein the ancient strictures of Hindutva it is said that sanyasis cannot marry and have wives. Wives are addressed by the name Dharmapatne meaning consort in Dharma bringing in solemnity in the family life manifesting by the coming together of males and females. So the quintessence of the whole effort is to substantiate the reality that it's the males and females who are entitled to naturally come around unite and become families and not unnatural gay people of same-sex causing unnatural union and adversities bringing in warth of nature in the form of catastrophes of immense rise in crimes, pandemic, and blizzards. In 100 A D Rome legalized gay sex and the malady and ravage of adharmic activities perpetrating decadence and ravage of humanity was stultified and arrested by the law of death sentence to gays in the medieval eras. This is Dharma in life's ways as Karma in reality. Now we are in modern times and have gained great knowledge so as not to award death sentences to gays who by misfortune and unfortunate turn of event in their lives was forced or by incessant abuse made to before in their dispositions. We are equipped with medical facilities for curing these maladies and bringing back these unfortunate humans to mainstream social life through proper medical care and treatment by psychologists and psychiatrists. Anyone and everyone caught in these unnatural activities should be compulsorily made to undergo treatment so as to cure them of these maladies and bring them back to mainstream social life.Transgender rights have been first recognized and propagated by The Honorable Supreme court of India.Unfortunately, Transgenders are seen clubbed with gays .. The gays reap in the benefits of transgender's grouping with them. Actually are Transgenders really Gayas is the cardinal question. Naturally, Transgenders are neither males nor females that is they do not come within the genders. So they are classified as the third gender. Transgenders are naturally handicapped and usually do not have gay attitudes. If one goes by realities gays abuse transgenders for sex and sodomy creating mental trauma and exploiting them. Nowadays one finds males growing breasts and after growing breasts using hormones etc, they style themselves as Trangenders going about exploiting ladies and gents alike. The same is being done by ladies who retards breasts and grow their clitoris going about saying that they are male transgenders. Then comes the passive partners of homosexuals who by constant abuse fo anal and other ways of homosexual activities assume the role of a female or dormant homosexual partners acquiring int the process female like attitudes of shyness coyness etc .These are all instances of males and females acquiring mental attitudes toward the opposite sex artificially. These mental attitudes and bodily changes are not sufficient to make people transgenders but unfortunately for exploitation, these not so good attituded people assume these roles ringing in water downing of the rights by abuse and exploitation.Clubbing

Transgenders along with gays is fraudulent and encourages only exploitation of the hapless naturally handicapped people.

" Belief" is of paramount importance and its belief that people themselves to go ahead in all ways. Ceasers wife is beyond suspicion is a belief but is it worth to believe like this is a question the answer to which has to be such so as to enable Humans to achieve successes in every spear they venture into on beliefs. You will hear people saying, You should believe me fully and completely, etc etc . is this possible, and even if it's possible whether it will take us to the desired levels of prominence in success. For upholding and sustaining Truth, happiness, progress, and success No one should believe anything except after rubbing it on the touchstone of intelligence, perception, Experience, and reasoning. Only if this is adhered to strictly one will come in Triumph untouched by deceit, cheating, and fraud. Reasoning power is a God bestowed power in Humans enabling us to decipher and detect Truth from falsities enabling humanity to Believe truthful realities and things augmenting progress in peace prosperity and happiness to lofty yonder heights. For acting on a belief The necessity is whether the belief is on realities and whether it's good for oneself and humanity in general. Learning these are simple tasks. Just watch and be awake to the innumerable experiences of oneself in life. Sharpen one's senses, intelligence, and powers of perception and have an open attitude with an open mind so as to be ready to perceive the secrets and necessities of natural manifestations good for humanity mainly by linking oneself with Dharmica ways and means of one's Soul and seeing to it that one never stray from the Dharma in lives ways as Karma. One will be alive to effectively know and perceive the immense knowledge abundantly available in nature's ways and dispositions and the reality that nature is ever willing to provide and allow the perception of the secrets and all-pervading realities on which it goes on and on. This way is the " Eshwara Guruveaa" way. After perceiving life's experiences just go for introspection as to the quintessence that crops up as a corollary from the endeavor rubbing it with one's life and life experiences so as to be aware of the realities. Lo one is unfurling the secrets of nature. One instance that comes to my mind is my son " Kunhee " making me understand without even his knowing that One has to listen and learn even from children so as to understand the significance of realities in life. Disagrements in life with people if properly dealt with with an open mind will result in discussions and reasoning leading to enlightenment for the benefit of oneself and others. There is an old saying that one has to listen to even children so as to become aware of realities in life's experiences enabling us to get enlightenment for our yonder Journeys in life. While my son Kunhee was about one and a half years old which was in 2011 sixth month. Myself and my now estranged separated wife were sitting on the sofa in our drawing room watching T V . I was on the western side sofa and my wife was on the Western side sofa My son Kunhee was on the middle sofa. While watching TV Kunhee started scratching me and my wife with his nails. We both scolded him and still, he went on scratching and blood started coming from my hand skin. On this, we both beat him and he started crying loudly. Then it suddenly dawned upon me Why not cut his nails. I and my wife took my baby son to the bathroom and started cutting his nails. I was astonished when he showed all his fingers without hesitation for cutting the nails. On finishing this nail cutting ..you should know what this young man did,, He said now everything is over and for this, you beat me up ..? I was rather overcome with remorse and shame on my automatically coming to know in my mind assuming what this young man meant was. My Father and Mother you people without doing your duty of cutting my nails why are you beating me up. Hope this will be enough to substantiate the old saying that One has to learn even from children to know of the secrets in nature for common good. Here we are delinquent of dereliction of our duty of cutting the nail of my son in time properly resulting in scratching and all and we are beating Kunhee up for our own faults. Wah what wonderful natural God's ways and means of Nature teaching humans.

While looking back on life's ways and experiences On comes across many instances which justify adhering to Dharma in life for proper and happy living.These w2hen properly evaluated and deciphered in the context of personification for future Dharma in life's ways as Karma, invigorates oneself as well as others inspiring all to strictly adhere to Dharma in life for achieving sustainable happiness.An instance coming to my mind in which I am myself involved is rather disturbing but bringing out the Dharmic as well as the evil ways resorted to by persons who get near to oneself as profound friends sabotaging oneself and others for some worthless advantages. These provide an opportunity for introspection and correction leading to invigorate and a relentless adherence to the correct Righteous God paved Dharmic ways in life's ways and means in one's journey of life. Furthering streamlining the necessity of compulsory substantiating adhering to Dharma in Karma of life's ways for trying to fulfill the purpose and aim of being born as a human being. I was a Junior independent Advocate practicing Civil, Criminal, Consumer, Motor accident, Citizenship, etc cases bringing in opportunities to deal with Indian constitutional matters and writs as is enshrined in the constitution of India as a remedy for wrongs involving violations of law or legal rights.Even at that time, my concept of an ideal Advocate both as an Advocate as well as a Human being was answered by The Greatest Advocate of all times our Late Advocate K.Kunhirama Menon. I was rather charmed and mesmerized by the legal Acumen of K.Kunhiram Menon and used to follow this great man whenever I could so as to enable me to watch The greatest Advocate in action in ways of conducting cases which were nunth available anywhere except when Mr. Kunhirama Menon was in action in courts. For Mr. Kunhirama Menon conducting murder cases was child's play and the usual and cross-examination of witnesses was sooo superbly good and incomparable that one won't find anyone as superb as Mr. Kunhiram Menon in these spears. Apart from cross-examination Mr. Kunhirama Menon\s, knowledge of law was explicitly fantastic combined with this drafting of factual propositions igniting manifestation of legal principles inherently; brought about the incomparable greatness of he Man as a complete advocate par excellence giving him a place of standing above all at an unreachable lofty height unachievable till now by anyone. In the witness box when Mr. Kunhirama Menon finishes cross-examination of a forensic expert Doctor who gets into the witness box with an insolence as to what this Old man is going to do to me gets bewildered and shattered bringing in a reality that forces one to believe and decide that the Doctor knows nothing and Mr Kunhirama Menon knows all and the doctor has blundered and is unbelievable. I was actually close to this Advocate and used to get excellent accommodation whenever I happened to be at or near Mr. Kunhirama Menon whatever the others say of or do to my detriment.Actually, I was close to many Juniors of this great Advocates office and was a constant visitor in the office. Of course, I was not a full-time Junior as is other Juniors in the offices.James Joseph Saviour George etc were my classmates in law who were attached to this office. When the famous Sub Inspector of Police Soman murder case came up in the Honorable High Court of Kerala in Appeal I expressed a desire to Mr. Kunhiram Menon and got permission to watch conducting of Murder Appeal cases in High court. In this Soman murder case the accused\s were all convicted by the Sessions Court to undergo life imprisonment and in The Appeal, before the High court of Kerala The two Justices' Divison bench differed in the decision and the matter was referred to the Full Bench and the matter was before the Full bench of The high court of Kerala comprising of Justice K.T Thomas sitting in the middle and Justice Thulais das and Justices Shamshuddin sitting on either side. Wow, it was a Majestic court. I presented myself in court by accompanying James Joseph Junior of Mr. Kunahiram Menon as it was the first time I ventured into the Honorable High court of Kerala.On entering the court hall I felt a sense of something being wrong anyway I entered the court and stood there The Justices were not on the dais as the court has not started sitting. James Joseph went ahead a step in front of me and showed some sign language communications I do not know what it is but immediately the senior Advocate Mr M.K.Damodharan fondly took K.Kunhirama Menon to the side behind a long curtain in the back I heard him murmuring do not allow Gadhadharan to sit in the front row of chairs in court. I looked back and saw Mr. Ramakrishnan Nair the son-in-law of Mr. Kunhirama Menon, sitting on the bench put up abutting the back sidewall of the court and gesturing to me to sit there at the back. I impulsively moved forward a step on this I heard Mr. Kunhirama Menon shouting with placing his foot strongly on the floor with a Sound, saying " He is an Advocate and can sit anywhere ".I was asked to sit in the front row next to Junior James joseph who was assisting in the case. I was given all files to peruse and learn.I sat in front and watched the Greatest Advocate smartly and easily not just conducting the case but winning the appeal and the court acquitting the accused giving them the benefit of doubt. I was thunderstruck by the magnanimity and humanness of Mr. Kunhiram Menon The sense of Dharm in Justice that was there in The great Human being's actions of whatever others feel or say one has to stick to Dharma in Justice to all. I am not even a junior and I got permission from, Mr. Kunhiram Menon, with great effort and think of it in spite of opposition from all even Juniors I was allowed to sit in the front row. Incomparable in Dharmic ways Mr. Kunhiram Menon whatever hankey Pankey ways were acted when it comes to realities and decision making it just Dharmic ways and means for this Greatest All-time personifiable Advocate.The humanness and sense of Justice in equality imparted and upheld by Late K.Kunhirama Menon is an enviable unattainable fit to be personified by all and everyone catapulting Mr. Kunhiram Menon to a level of prominence unachievable or unachieved by anyone. Mr. Kunhiram Menon went on conducting cases left and right until his unfortunate death or is it an untimely foul play death in his ninety-fourth year of par excellence as an Advocate as well as a human being.These are Dharma in life's Ways as Karma personifiable meant for and catapulting humanity to lofty yonder levels of prominence and humanness. This is what is humanness and what is intended by God as Dharma in life's ways as Karma pure and simple emanating from the inner elections of the unfathomable depths of one's heart reaching on to oneself and all is the soul's voice.

Think of it and ascertain the factual revelations of the quality of people Placing Mr. K.Kunhirama Menon with the conduct of my 30/9/2016 estranged separated wife my supposed Dharampathnee a supposed richest lady in Calicut incognito marrying me at the instance of these gangsters headed by these criminal-minded Judicial ruffian officers bent on sabotaging my carrier and profession by denying me work to earn a living intending to cause my death by starvation or slavery under them. This lady told me that I like I love you and am ready to marry you. Why do you worry I am here for you. We will get over all and thrive in life don't worry. I was really overawed by happiness and touched I Thought after all I have found someone who loves me that makes eighty percent success the rest twenty percent is some money. After all, if I get some cases as work I will manage much more than necessary. So I informed my Mother and eldest uncle and got them to mediate and married this supposed noble lady at the Kadalai Sree Krishan temple, Kannur, Kerala State. After marriage, its was fine except for some misgivings. Everything ok she became pregnant and a boy was born my son. After delivery, she started to go astray, especially with poisonous substances in food and creating cruel treatment of my son like sending this three-year-old to the neighbor pedophile an eighty-four-year man shorty with big narcfissic=st attributes causing me to notify my supposed in-laws who came and took her to their supposed house four times saying let her be there at Kannur and she will be alright. On the last time, my supposed Dharmpatni was at her in-law's people came to my house warning me that my son will be killed and begged me to somehow save my son from peril. I contacted a retired Assistant Commissioner of Sales tax who is also a C P I (M) activist and went to Kannur there were lots of people who talked My wife answered that she will never poison food and is coming with me to live properly. I didn't go further and got her back to my house. It was ok except that she wanted this Sudhir Judge to come above all and told me that she will listen to only Sudhir. Then she said that Razhil is all-important here around and should come up in life not me it seems. I retorted maybe he is but here in my house I am important Only these misgivings were there. Unfortunately suddenly on 28/9/16, she poisoned my food to such an extent that it was horrible driving me to the verge of death but fortunately I escaped. I was flabbergasted and asked her why she is doing this to me and what if I die. She retorted Why don't you die you are sixty. I did not do anything just called her supposed folks and apprised them of this diabolical activity. That day I and my son slept in my bedroom and asked her to sleep in the other bedroom in which my son sleeps now. On 30/9/2016 my supposed inlaws with one Vinodh came by car and took her from my house. She was seen in the neighbor's house of mine that evening itself. My son refuses to go with his mother for fear of being killed and harmed. Since that time in 2016, I am living in my ancestral house with my son. Now he is going to be twelve in July. I later learned that she is a member of these gangsters headed by criminal-minded Judicial officers and close to Sudhir Judge. Why they are after me I don't know but my supposed Dharmapatnee is siding with these antisocials and behaving in a diabolically ruffian manner and attempting to kill me is rampantly clear. I don't know why. Comrades evaluate the diverse and opposite attitudes of two Human beings and come to your own conclusions as to the quality of their psychophysical mechanisms in relation to Dharma in life's ways as Karma.

Comrades, it's not just the Oral utterances and physical appearance of a person that is important but the mental attitudes deep within manifesting in perils and turbulent situations. Mental attitudes one cant perceive easily except when confronted with instances and incidents cropping up in life's ways, especially in perilous and damaging situations driving oneself to the verge of death and destruction. Whatever be the oral declarations and utterances. It's the combination of mental attitudes as well as that of the physical manifestations of an individual or person that is namely the Psychophysical mechanism that determines the quality of an individual in life or class of one's personality. In evaluating the totality of dispositions and situations one comes to the inescapable reality that No one or a human being is entitled to do anything that will bring in harm to others in the exercise of freedoms guaranteed bringing in inconveniences bad effects and miseries except when it's for common good justifiable by truth and reality. Humanity, in general, is concerned with any deeds activities, and dispositions of a single Human being if it affects the well being welfare, and Good of others or humanity in general. As even the deeds dispositions aims aspirations and activities of a single human being affect humanity in general the necessity of formulating laws for the good of all springs up and is catered to by the enacting of laws in legislatures by people's representatives for the people's good after great debates deliberations and public opinions. Laws are the crystallization of the principles expressing the will of people for their good intended to secure and achieve progress of humanity in peace. prosperity and happiness accentuating the necessity and need for all to go by laws thereby streamlining and hastening the ultimate quantum leap contemplated to the Era of the rule of Love . Nowadays one finds even Judicial officers sidelining and ignoring legal principles while passing orders on the pretext of practicality and convenience. To suppress a provision for some things that need to be taken into consideration before coming to a conclusion is what is deceit and fraud. These types of fraudulent practices are ravaging the trust of the judiciary in all nations, especially in India where a report by Transparency International says that about more than seventy percent of the people do not trust the Judiciary. Rule of law is said to be consistent certain and uniform applying to all alike. When Judicial officers suppress facts and law while arriving at findings it's the Judiciary itself causing an implosion perpetrating uncertainty and chaos creating a distrust that nothing is certain in legal circles. Only emphasizing that achieving "Theoretical perfection practically achieved is the best that can be ever achieved" concept in all matters relating to Rule of law will enable solving these maladies gnawing at the root of the administration of justice bringing in distrust of the judiciary in the minds of all. Like the laws of science Rule of law should all be applied uniformly and consistently always in all situations otherwise The concept of rule of law will also lose all significance and bring in the opposite effect as is in the case of scientific laws when stopped for a moment. Think of ti the law of gravitational stopping for a minute Ho can't imagine all will be lost. Dharm in present times is Rule of law especially as its profused to be for good of all treating all equally and giving equal protection to all. Adharmic deeds in any form by anyone even under the pretext of exercising one's freedoms should be nipped in the bud as it impinges upon the progress in peace prosperity and happiness of humanity.

Gadhadharan Punathil

In conclusion, one is confronted with a peculiar reality that in matters of life's ways and means of activities in deeds culminating in prominence and achievements one is the sole Judge Jury investigator collecting all evidence of facts and dispositions perceiving evaluating all. Testing all on the touchstone of reasoning and reality thereby deciding for oneself as to what is right and good. It is the quality in accordance with the realities of one's decisions that ignites and kindles the progress so as to enable the scaling of the yonder lofty heights ascendable by anyone. In short, all depends on the quality of a human being closely intermingled in capacities and capabilities of perceiving the secrets of nature for one's own good as well as the common good of humanity. The endeavor of ascertaining The Dharma's ways as is manifested and ascertainable from the experiences of humanity's Journey whereby Dharmic ways in life are stultified deciphered asserted and practicalized are matters being solely left in the perceptive powers and reasoning of persons in perceiving assimilating realizing accepting adopting and making practical these concepts as is unfurled as " Dharma in life's Ways as Karma" in the course of one's as well as humanity's life's Journies. Ultimately The enlightenment dawns upon oneself that what is good need not make oneself happy But it's best to go for that which is good for oneself and humanity at large not for momentary happiness later on turning sour pushing oneself and humanity into unhappiness and chaos. Its ways for sustainable happiness progress in prosperity and peace that one has to look for perceive accept adapt and achieve. Momentary happiness and progress later turning bad and bringing in adverse effects have to be eschewed by using ones God bestowed powers of senses perception intelligence reasoning and ultimately The voice of the soul.

Gadhadharan Punathil
Punathil house
Manipuram lane
Nadakav
Calicut-673011
Kerala State
India

9 798886 843880

Printed by Libri Plureos GmbH in Hamburg, Germany